1900—1919

Yearbooks in Science

1900–1919

Tom McGowen

Twenty-First Century Books
A Division of Henry Holt and Company
New York

Twenty-First Century Books
A Division of Henry Holt and Company, Inc.
115 West 18th Street
New York, NY 10011

Henry Holt® and colophon are trademarks of Henry Holt and Company, Inc.
Publishers since 1866

Published in Canada by Fitzhenry & Whiteside Ltd.
195 Allstate Parkway, Markham, Ontario L3R 4T8

Library of Congress Cataloging-in-Publication Data
Yearbooks in science.
p. cm.
Includes indexes.
Contents: 1900–1919 / Tom McGowen — 1920–1929 / David E. Newton — 1930–1939 / Nathan Aaseng —
1940–1949 / Nathan Aaseng — 1950–1959 / Mona Kerby — 1960–1969 / Tom McGowen — 1970–1979 /
Geraldine Marshall Gutfreund — 1980–1989 / Robert E. Dunbar — 1990 and beyond / Herma Silverstein.
ISBN 0–8050–3431–5 (v. 1)
1. Science—History—20th century—Juvenile literature. 2. Technology—History—20th century—Juvenile
literature. 3. Inventions—History—20th century—Juvenile literature. 4. Scientists—20th century—Juvenile
literature. 5. Engineers—20th century—Juvenile literature. [1. Science—History—20th century.
2. Technology—History—20th century.]
Q126.4.Y43 1995   95–17485
609'.04—dc20   CIP
                                                    AC

ISBN 0–8050–3431–5
First Edition 1995
Printed in Mexico
All first editions are printed on acid-free paper ∞.
10 9 8 7 6 5 4 3 2 1

Cover design by James Sinclair
Interior design by Kelly Soong

Cover photo credits
Background: *Tyrannosaurus rex*, Neg. No. 315109/Courtesy Department Library Services/American Museum
of Natural History. **Inset images** (clockwise from top center): Hertzsprung-Russell diagram, Courtesy the
Harvard/Smithsonian Center for Astrophysics; pollen, Dr. Jeremy Burgess/Science Photo Library/Photo
Researchers, Inc.; image representing time, The Fourth Dimension, created by James Sinclair; nuclear atom,
Mehau Kulyk, SPL/Photo Researchers, Inc.; woolly mammoth, Trans. No. 2431/Painting by C. R.
Knight/Courtesy Department Library Services/AMNH; trilobite, Neg. No. K13081/Photograph by Jim
Cox/Courtesy Department Library Services/AMNH.

Photo credits
p. 11, 13, 19, 32, 52: Science Photo Library/Photo Researchers, Inc.; p. 16, 21, 30, 73: The Bettmann Archive; p.
18: Dr. Jeremy Burgess/SPL/Photo Researchers, Inc.; p. 23: Mehau Kulyk/SPL/Photo Researchers, Inc.; p. 25:
AIP Emilio Segrè Visual Archives; p. 26, 42: Dr. Fred Espenak/SPL/Photo Researchers, Inc.; p. 33: Bob
Pizaro/Comstock, Inc.; p. 38: Harvard College Observatory; p. 47: Larry Mulvehill/Photo Researchers, Inc.; p. 50:
National Museum of Health & Medicine/Armed Forces Institute of Pathology; p. 55: Courtesy of the Archives,
California Institute of Technology; p. 58: Trans. No. 2431/Painting by C.R. Knight/Courtesy Department Library
Services/American Museum of Natural History; p. 60: Neg. No. 293067/Photograph by Lilo Hess/Courtesy
Department Library Services/AMNH; p. 61: Neg. No. 315109/Courtesy Department Library Services/AMNH; p.
66: Neg. No. K13081/Photograph by Jim Coxe/Courtesy Department Library Services/AMNH; p. 68:
Paleogeographic Atlas Project/David Rowley/University of Chicago; p. 76: NASA/Mark Marten/Photo
Researchers, Inc.

For Erin and Sean

Contents

1

PHYSICS

Physics is the science that seeks to find the causes of natural things, such as wind, lightning, gravity, or the glow of the sun. As the last ten years of the nineteenth century began, a great many physicists truly believed that virtually all the causes of most of these things had been discovered. They felt that "classical" physics—the answers that had been worked out by the great seventeenth-century English scientist Isaac Newton and other early physicists—covered just about everything, and there were no more mysteries left to be solved.

Then, suddenly, there was an explosion of *new* mysteries. Incredible new discoveries demanded answers:

- A French physicist named Antoine Becquerel found that the metal uranium gave off mysterious rays that went through paper, glass, and thin aluminum, and would darken photographic film just as sunlight does. What could cause such "radioactivity" to be given off by a lifeless metal?

- An Englishman named J. J. Thomson reported that a stream of radiation created by electricity generated into a glass tube was apparently made up of parts of atoms. But atoms were supposed to be indivisible and indestructible. How could they be giving off parts of themselves?

- Physicists measuring the frequency of light waves given off by a heated, glowing object found that their measurements simply didn't agree with what classical physics said they ought to be. What was the reason?

So, as the twentieth century dawned, many physicists were trying to find the answers to these and other mysteries. The answers they found actually changed the world.

PACKAGES OF LIGHT

In 1900, a German physicist named Max Planck made one of the most important discoveries in the history of the science of physics. But he hated it! He spent much of the rest of his life trying to prove that it was wrong!

Planck loved the science of physics. He particularly loved "classical" physics: the laws and ideas established mainly by Isaac Newton. Therefore, Planck was unhappy about something that a number of physicists had discovered during the last part of the nineteenth century, because it seemed to contradict classical physics. This discovery concerned the way that light was apparently radiated (given off) by a glowing hot object.

According to classical physics, an object such as a chunk of metal heated white-hot in a furnace gave off waves of light, like the ripples in a pool of water spreading out from the point where a stone was dropped in. Classical physics also implied that the energy (heat and light) from such a heated object could be given off in any amount, continuously. But when some physicists worked out an experiment for measuring the energy given off by a heated object, they found that what classical physics had said was apparently quite wrong!

Physicists measured radiating energy with what was called a blackbody. Originally, a blackbody was just an imaginary concept that physicists used for working out ideas, but some physicists actually built one for some radiation experiments. It was simply a hollow metal ball, perfectly black inside and out, with a small hole in it. When the ball was heated in an oven, it soon began to glow, giving off light from both the outside and inside, through the hole. The physicists measured the radiation by making a chart that recorded the increase in the light's brightness and color as the temperature increased. However, the measurement showed that the blackbody did not give off energy continuously in any quantity at all, as the mathematics of classical physics said it should. Instead, the radiation reached a peak, then grew less, in what the chart showed as a downward curve.

Max Planck couldn't accept this. He felt that something must have been overlooked. So he began to work on the problem. He did it with mathematics, trying to produce an equation that would show exactly what was happening during blackbody radiation. He hoped the formula might reveal what was going wrong with previous radiation experiments.

Planck spent months coming up with one set of calculations after another, and getting nowhere. Finally, he decided to throw out most of what he had done and come at things from another angle. Instead of assuming that classical physics was automatically right, he began to work from the idea that maybe something thought to be impossible was happening as a blackbody radiated energy. And suddenly, his mathematics began to fit together.

When Planck finally finished his work, he was disappointed to see that it seemed to prove that the blackbody experiment results were absolutely right. His mathematics showed that light was not being released in waves, as classical physics stated, but was actually being given off as little spurts of energy in "packages."

This was the impossibility Planck had been working with, and he could scarcely believe it. He didn't want to believe it! But he named the tiny energy packages quanta, from the Latin word *quantum*, meaning "how much," and announced his discovery for other physicists to consider. Many of them thought his finding was ridiculous, for there seemed to be a great deal of evidence showing that light definitely moved in waves.

However, during the next few years some other physicists made use of Max Planck's discovery to help solve problems they were working on, and they found that the quanta idea provided sound answers to certain puzzling mysteries. Eventually, the concept of quanta became the basis for a whole new branch of physics known as quantum physics, which investigates the tiny world of atoms and their particles. In 1918, Max

Max Planck's theory of light quanta laid the foundation for quantum physics.

Planck was awarded the Nobel Prize in physics for his work in putting together the quantum theory of light.

THE EIGHTEEN-HUNDRED-MILE MESSAGE

On December 12, 1901, a man in a little town on the coast of England prepared to tap out the three dots of the letter *S* in Morse code. Eighteen hundred miles (3,000 kilometers) across the Atlantic Ocean, in Newfoundland, Canada, other men bent over an electrical apparatus and waited. The first attempt at international radio communication was about to be made.

The first steps toward this important experiment had been taken twenty-eight years earlier, in 1873. Scottish physicist James Maxwell had presented the idea that an alternating (changing) electric current would cause a magnetic field, producing electromagnetic radiation that would flow through the air in waves. In 1885, Heinrich Hertz of Germany conducted an experiment to see if he could create such waves. He constructed a device that produced an alternating current and caused a spark to appear in another device a short distance away. This proved that electromagnetic waves could be created and that they would travel through the air.

In 1894, after Hertz's death, a popular magazine carried an article about his work. A twenty-year-old Italian by the name of Guglielmo Marconi picked up a copy of the magazine and read the article. Marconi was a tinkerer and inventor as well as a physicist, and he was suddenly dazzled by the realization that the waves Hertz had produced could be used to transmit messages over a long distance, using the dot and dash signals of Morse code. The best way of sending such messages at that time was by telegraph—a means of

---

WHAT IS A THEORY?

Max Planck created what is called the quantum theory, and you have probably also heard of Einstein's theory of relativity and Darwin's theory of evolution. Many of the things that scientists write are called theories. But just what *is* a theory?

Many people think that *theory* means "guess" or "idea," but that isn't at all correct. In science, *theory* means "an explanation for something that is known to happen, or that has happened." In other words, it is an explanation for a *fact* or facts that are not always fully understood. A theory has to be based upon careful study, logical thinking, a good understanding of science, and actual *evidence*. Guesswork plays no part in any scientific theory.

sending electrical impulses through wires. But telegraph communication required miles of wires strung between upright poles. With electromagnetic waves, no wires would be needed. It was unbelievable to Marconi that no one else had thought of this.

He quickly went to work. Within a month, he was able to make electromagnetic waves ring a bell 30 feet (9 meters) away from his transmitting device. Within a year, he was sending waves more than 1 mile (1.6 kilometers). (Because electromagnetic waves are a form of radiation, they became known as radio waves.)

At the turn of the twentieth century, Marconi was sending dot and dash signals as far as 30 miles (48 kilometers). By now, he had attracted the attention of many scientists. Their opinions were not at all encouraging. They predicted that communication by means of radio waves would not be possible for more than a few hundred miles because of the curvature of the earth. If the waves reached as far as where the earth began to curve away under them, these scientists explained, the waves would simply fly on out into space.

Marconi intended to see for himself, however. He had a large transmitter (device for sending radio waves) put together at the town of Poldu, in Cornwall, England. Then he sailed to Newfoundland and set up a receiver in

Guglielmo Marconi, the discoverer of radio transmission, often built his own instruments.

the coastal town of Saint John's. On December 12, when the three dots were tapped out in England, they were heard almost instantly in Newfoundland. Marconi had proved that long-distance radio communication of the kind that now links our world together was possible, despite what many scientists had said.

It was later discovered that the other scientists had actually been right. Radio waves do fly out into space. But when they hit a part of the atmosphere known as the ionosphere, they are reflected back down to earth and can be picked up by receivers. Marconi's stubborn determination to carry out his experiment gave scientists the opportunity to learn about the reflective properties of the ionosphere, which otherwise might not have been discovered until much later. In 1909, Guglielmo Marconi received the Nobel Prize (shared with Karl Braun of Germany) for his work on "wireless telegraphy," or radio.

Solving the Mystery of Radioactivity

It was just about time for the 1901 Christmas vacation to begin at McGill University, in Montreal, Canada, and two men were straightening up the laboratory where they had been working during the year. Ernest Rutherford, who was a professor of physics at the university, and Frederick Soddy, who taught chemistry, had been working together in their spare time, trying to solve the mystery of radioactivity, the strange radiation of energy that had been discovered coming from certain metals.

When Antoine Becquerel had announced his discovery that the metal uranium gave off radiation, Rutherford was one of the physicists who became eager to find out what this radiation was, and what was causing it. Uranium, radium, polonium, and thorium, the metals known to be radioactive, seemed to be ordinary metals just like iron or lead, so how could they be giving off invisible rays that would go through certain kinds of materials, would darken photographic film, and would burn human skin? For such things to happen, there had to be light and heat, but for light and heat to be present, there had to be something producing energy, such as a fire. There was certainly no fire inside a chunk of metal, so where was the energy coming from?

Rutherford had begun trying to find the answer to that question by measuring the radioactivity of uranium, to learn exactly how much energy was being produced. He was astonished to find that it was quite a large amount—more than any ordinary chemical process, such as burning, could produce. This made Rutherford wonder if perhaps something was happening in the atoms that formed the uranium. This was a wild idea, because classical physics taught that atoms were simply solid, inert building blocks that couldn't possibly "do" anything.

Rutherford began to study the radioactive metal thorium, and soon detected that it was giving off what seemed to be a radioactive gas, which he named thorium emanation. Investigating the gas, he found that its radioactivity got weaker as time passed, until there was hardly any at all. By keeping a careful record of the radioactivity, he was able to learn that it lost exactly half its strength every fifty-four seconds. He named this weakening process "half-life," to indicate that the "life" of the radioactivity was constantly being reduced by half.

It was at this point that Rutherford and Soddy joined forces. Rutherford wanted to find out more about thorium emanation, and decided he needed to work with a chemist. So he asked Soddy to help him. Soddy made a chemical analysis, and found that the gas was not at all like thorium; it was actually a different element (an element is a substance formed of only one kind of atom), and its atoms were completely different from those of thorium. This was a gigantic puzzle! Where could these new atoms have possibly come from?

Next, Soddy used a chemical process to remove the thorium itself from the rocky material it was mixed with. He and Rutherford were astonished to find that the pure thorium was just barely radioactive, while the material it had been taken from was very radioactive. Was it the rocky material that was actually producing all the radiation, and not the thorium?

With the Christmas holiday at hand, there was simply no time to begin investigating this. So the two men put the highly radioactive material into a container, labeled it "thorium X," closed up the laboratory, and left. When they returned two weeks later, the first thing they did was check the thorium and thorium X to see if there had been any change in them. Rutherford and Soddy were thunderstruck to find that the thorium, which had been only weakly radioactive when they left, was now giving off powerful radiation. But the thorium X, which had been strongly radioactive, was now hardly radioactive at all! What could this mean?

Frederick Soddy's chemical research helped to solve the mystery of radiation.

The two men had an idea of what it might mean. Perhaps thorium X, like thorium emanation, had a half-life, and most of its radioactivity was now gone. Testing their theory, they found that this was exactly right. Thorium X indeed had a half-life, of four weeks, and chemical analysis showed that it, too, was completely different from thorium. Furthermore, Soddy found that it was thorium X that gave off thorium emanation, not the pure thorium.

Now, all the clues were coming together and the two scientists were able to figure things out. What was happening was that thorium was constantly turning into thorium X and thorium X was constantly becoming thorium emanation. Only one more piece was needed to solve the puzzle, and Rutherford found that in 1902, when he determined that the radiation given off by thorium was nothing less than particles (tiny parts) of atoms.

Rutherford had solved the mystery of radioactivity. In 1903, he announced his findings to the scientists of the world. Radioactivity, he told them, was the energy being released by the breaking up of atoms. It was caused by tiny particles literally tearing loose from an atom and speeding away as microscopic "sparks" of heat and light. And when an atom lost a certain number of particles, Rutherford explained, it was no longer an atom of the same kind; it became a totally different element. He showed that many radioactive substances are actually just changed versions of one another. For example, uranium loses particles until it becomes radium, which loses particles until it becomes polonium, and polonium loses particles until it becomes lead, which is no longer radioactive.

Just as Max Planck had discovered something that was supposed to be impossible, so had Rutherford and Soddy. They had discovered that atoms were not the inert, inactive objects classical physics had declared them to be.

Atoms could change. Some of them could change into something completely different, by losing bits of themselves in the form of radiation. This discovery played an enormous part in our understanding of atoms. In 1908, Ernest Rutherford was awarded the Nobel Prize in chemistry for his studies of radioactive substances and his discovery of how atoms break up. In 1921, Frederick Soddy received the Nobel Prize in chemistry for his work on radioactive substances and certain types of atoms.

EINSTEIN ASTOUNDS THE SCIENTIFIC WORLD

In 1905, no one had ever heard of Albert Einstein. He was nothing more than a twenty-six-year-old office worker in the city of Bern, Switzerland. As a schoolboy, Einstein had been considered "slow" by most of his teachers, who felt he would never amount to much.

But Albert Einstein was enchanted with mathematics and was a deep, logical thinker. In college, he studied mathematics and physics and became what is known as a theoretical physicist—a physicist who does most of his or her work in the mind, rather than in a laboratory. His office work gave him time to do a great deal of thinking, and he slowly worked out answers to a number of physics problems that interested him. During 1905, he sent a German science magazine several articles that presented his solutions to things he had been working on.

The first of these articles, published shortly after his twenty-sixth birthday, dealt with what was known as the photoelectric effect. This was the name for a discovery the physicist Hertz had made while working with radio waves—that a metal surface gives off a small amount of electricity if a light shines on it. Scientists could not explain why this happened.

But Einstein had worked it out. While many scientists were not sure whether light was formed of waves or particles, Einstein showed that light is *formed* of tiny packages, as Max Planck had discovered, and that these packages *travel* in waves. He explained that a package of light (later called a photon) had so much energy and traveled so fast that when it struck metal, it could actually knock an electron out of one of the metal's atoms. When a number of electrons were "knocked loose" in this way, they produced an electric current.

Thus, Einstein had not only solved the puzzle of the photoelectric effect, he had also solved the vexing problem of whether light was waves or particles by showing that it behaves like both. On the scientific side, this work of Einstein's helped establish the science of quantum mechanics, which investigates the structure and behavior of atoms and the motion of atomic particles. On the technological side, the work helped lead to the invention of sound motion pictures and television.

Another of Einstein's articles helped prove the existence of atoms. Despite the discoveries that had been made about atoms and molecules (clusters of atoms), there were still some scientists who were not sure that atoms really existed. Some even insisted that science had no business trying to investigate things that were invisible and couldn't be measured, weighed, or counted. But Einstein showed how the atoms that form liquids *could* be measured.

To do this, he made use of a discovery made nearly eighty years earlier by a Scottish botanist. This man, Robert Brown, had found that when microscopic grains of pollen from plants were floating in liquid, they were constantly jiggling, bouncing, and dancing, like tiny energetic animals. In time, it was found that any extremely tiny particle suspended in liquid does this same constant jiggling dance, which became known as Brownian motion. Up to Einstein's time, no one could explain why this happened.

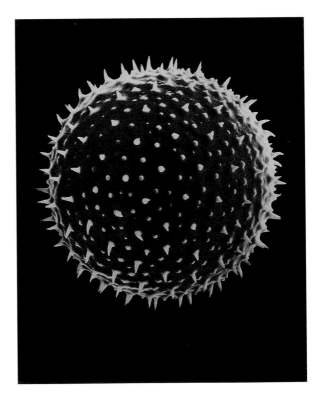

Scientists had worked out that while atoms forming a solid are tightly bound together (which is *why* the matter they form is a solid), those that form a liquid move around (which is why the substance is a liquid). Einstein explained that any tiny solid object such as a grain of pollen, suspended in a liquid, is going to be bumped and pushed around by

Even something so simple as a single grain of pollen, shown here magnified many times, played a part in proving the existence of atoms.

the motion of the atoms all around it. Objects that are bigger than the atoms won't get pushed as hard or as far, but those closer to an atom's size will get jostled quite a bit. Einstein showed how it would be possible to measure the average distance that different-sized particles in liquid moved during a particular period of time, which would show how hard and how often they were getting pushed. From this, by means of mathematics, the size of the atoms making up the liquid could be estimated—they could be measured. So, in this case, Einstein not only showed how atoms could be measured, and thus proved to exist, but he also solved the mystery of Brownian motion—the particles jiggle because they're getting bumped by atoms.

Albert Einstein's contribution to twentieth-century science was enormous.

Einstein's third article, published on June 30, contained some of the deepest thinking in scientific history. The work is very hard for most people to understand because all of its ideas are presented in the symbols of higher mathematics. However, most of the things that it presented can be explained with examples.

The article was originally entitled "On the Electrodynamics of Moving Bodies," but the ideas it presented soon became known as the special theory of relativity. This was because it showed that such things as motion, speed, distance, and time are not unchangeable and firmly established, but are actually all *relative* to—that is, dependent upon—the situation of someone who is observing them. For example, a passenger in a jet airplane flying at hundreds of miles an hour is not really aware that the plane is moving. Unless there is bumping from air currents, the plane feels just about the same as when it is sitting motionless on the ground. But a person on the ground, watching the plane go by overhead, sees it rushing through the sky at great speed. The motion of the plane is relative to the observations of the two people in different places.

What this means is that some very strange things might be possible due to the way time and motion could be experienced in different places. For a person in a spaceship traveling at nearly the speed of light (186,262 miles [299,792 kilometers] a second) and for a person on earth, time would seem to be the same. But, as Einstein pointed out, light is the fastest thing in the universe, so time would actually be moving much faster for the spaceship than on earth. The person on the spaceship could come back to earth after a trip that seemed only a few weeks long to find that many *years* had gone by on earth! Einstein's mathematics indicated that this was possible.

Einstein had still another article dealing with relativity published in September of 1905. This one presented the tremendous discovery that matter, such as an atom of something, and energy—heat and light—are simply two forms of the same thing. This was shown in Einstein's now-famous mathematical formula $E = mc^2$, or "energy equals mass at the speed of light squared." It was this formula that indicated that if the mass of an atom could be converted into energy, a tremendous amount of energy would be the result. This knowledge eventually led to the atomic bomb, nuclear power plants, and nuclear engines.

Even after Einstein's articles were published, most ordinary people, and even most scientists, still knew nothing of him. But physicists who read his articles were astounded. Some could not agree with all of his ideas, but others were overwhelmed by what he had done. Max Planck said that after reading Einstein's theory of relativity, he felt that the whole world had changed.

Gradually, Einstein's ideas became better known. In 1921, he received the Nobel Prize for his contributions to mathematical physics and his explanation of the photoelectric effect.

THE SOUND TUBE

Lee De Forest, an American inventor and researcher in radio communication, produced what some people have called the greatest invention of the twentieth century.

De Forest began his work on the invention in 1899. At that time, one of the main parts of a radio receiving set was an instrument known as a Branley Coherer, which picked the sounds of a radio broadcast out of the radio waves carrying them. The coherer was a rather crude device—a metal tube filled with iron filings—and did not do a very good job. De Forest was trying to produce an instrument that would work far better.

Because of something that had once happened during an experiment he was doing, De Forest had the feeling that heat could help pick sound out of radio waves. He tried putting a gas flame between two electrical terminals, but the room he was in was drafty. To keep the flame from fluttering, De Forest put a glass covering over the flame and the terminals. This was too bulky, but it led him to the idea of using a heated glass tube. He constructed a kind of lightbulb with an electrode in it, heated by a glowing filament. Plugged into a radio receiving set, the bulb did pick up sound, but not any better than the Branley Coherer. However, De Forest felt he was on the right track.

Some kind of push or boost was needed. Over a period of time, De Forest tried putting strips of tinfoil and other metals between the filament and the electrode. At about midnight on New Year's Eve, 1906, he twisted a piece of platinum wire into a crude grid shape, like a section of window screen, and put it in place. When the tube was plugged in, De Forest was elated to hear, loud and clear, the voice of his assistant, speaking into a transmitter several rooms away.

De Forest thought he had simply produced a device for picking up sound, as he had set out to do. He called his invention an Audion Tube, using Latin words meaning "sound thing." But what he had actually made was what is now called an amplifier, which increases sounds coming into a radio receiver. Without this invention, long-distance radio communication would not have been possible except by using the clicks or buzzes of Morse

Lee De Forest's Audion Tube, the first amplifier, made long-distance radio communication possible.

code. It was also important to the later development of television, of course. Thus, Lee De Forest played a big part in shaping the kind of world we live in.

De Forest was also responsible for another invention that will probably always be with us. He was the person who made up the term *broadcast*.

THE INSIDE OF AN ATOM

Throughout the nineteenth century, physicists had thought of atoms as being somewhat like microscopic billiard balls—tiny hard lumps of matter that absolutely could not be broken apart. But then, J. J. Thomson discovered that atoms had smaller parts (which became known as electrons), and Rutherford and Soddy found that some atoms were shooting bits of themselves off in all directions and turning into something else. Thus, within the first few years of the twentieth century, scientists were aware that atoms were a great deal more complicated than had been thought. The big question was, how complicated? What was the structure of an atom?

There were several ideas. Thomson, an Englishman, thought that an atom might be somewhat like an English plum pudding! A plum pudding is a kind of roundish moist cake filled with raisins, and Thomson thought an atom might be a roundish ball of positive electricity filled with electrons. A German physicist, Philipp Lenard, had a very different idea. He thought an atom must be mostly just open space, with particles floating around in it in pairs.

But once again it was Ernest Rutherford who figured out what an atom is basically like. Rutherford, by then a professor at a college in England, put some of his students to work on a project to measure the speed of particles shot forth by the radioactive metal radium. To do this, they had a tiny bit of radium sitting inside a lead box with a very small hole in one end. Radioactive particles cannot get through lead, so particles could only get out of the box through the hole, in a thin, steady stream. Lined up with the hole, some distance away, was a sheet of glass coated with zinc sulfide, which gave off a tiny flash of light every time a particle hit it. With a steady stream of particles hitting this screen, it generally showed a constant pinpoint of light, indicating that the particles were coming straight at it.

But when Rutherford had his students start putting things between the hole in the box and the zinc sulfide screen, something puzzling happened. A piece of gold foil (a tissue-thin sheet of gold) would let most of the particles go straight through it as if it weren't even there, but sometimes a particle would veer off and strike the screen at an angle. It was as if these particles had bumped into something that knocked them off their straight path.

The gold foil was composed entirely of gold atoms, of course, so Rutherford knew that whatever was happening was the result of the *structure* of the atoms. The fact that most of the particles were going straight through the foil

Ernest Rutherford believed an atom's structure resembled planets orbiting the sun.

suggested to him that there must be a lot of empty space in the atoms, and the particles were simply whizzing right through it. But because a particle would sometimes bounce off at an angle, Rutherford reasoned that there must be some object in each atom that was bigger than a particle and that had a positive electrical charge, just as the particles did. Thus, if a particle passed close to this object, it would get pushed away—just as the positive poles of two magnets will push each other away—and would continue its flight at a slight angle.

What this made Rutherford think of was our solar system. The solar system has the huge sun in the center, with tiny planets circling around it within billions of miles of empty space. So Rutherford pictured an atom as having a "large" object in the center—a nucleus—with electrons spinning around it in orbits, like miniature planets, in a vast amount of emptiness.

Rutherford presented this idea in 1911. It utterly destroyed the old idea of atoms as "billiard balls" closely packed together to form substances. What it meant was that matter, even such "hard" matter as a piece of iron, is literally formed mostly of *emptiness*. By revealing atoms as such strange, empty things, Rutherford changed the whole world's way of thinking, from then on.

LEAPING ELECTRONS

Ernest Rutherford had given the world a picture of the structure of an atom. But his picture did not show how atoms did things, such as producing light and radiation. There were still a lot of questions to be answered.

Rutherford had a friend who was a young Danish physicist by the name of Niels Bohr. Bohr loved Rutherford's picture of the atom, but he wanted it to answer all the unanswered questions. So he went to work to revise it.

Rutherford's picture of the atom had electrons circling around the nucleus in orbits. But an electron doing that would sooner or later run out of energy and its orbit would slow down and begin spiraling in closer and closer to the nucleus. However, there was no evidence that this actually happened, so Bohr decided there must be something very special about an electron orbit that kept it steady. He found that if he applied Max Planck's quanta idea to the orbit, mathematics showed that electrons in an atom could travel only in regular, unchanging orbits and could never lose speed and slide into a different orbit. Bohr decided that electrons were like the light photons Einstein had described, formed of quanta of energy. The distance of an electron's orbit from the nucleus depended upon the amount of energy the electron possessed. The more energy, the farther out the orbit.

However, things could happen to make an electron "leap" from one orbit to another, Bohr determined. If a light photon or an electrically charged particle came speeding into the atom, an electron could literally steal some of its energy, and this extra energy would then cause it to jump out to the next farthest orbit, or to an even farther orbit, depending upon how much energy it had seized. But immediately, then, the electron would let go of a quantum (single "package") of its own energy, which would go shooting out of the atom in the form of a light photon. *This* was how atoms gave off light and radiation. When the electron released the quantum of energy, it then instantly

Niels Bohr astonished the world of physics with his ideas about electron orbits.

jumped back to the next lowest orbit. Bohr called these jumps of electrons "quantum leaps."

Niels Bohr presented his picture of an atom in 1913, and most physicists were astounded by it. The idea of leaping electrons and unchanging orbits seemed impossible, but these ideas certainly explained a lot of puzzling things. What Bohr's picture of the atom clearly showed was that in the tiny world of atoms, things can happen very differently from the way they might in the "big" world we live in.

Bohr's explanation of the atom's structure and behavior was not complete, and it contained some errors. But it is the basis for our understanding of the atom today. For his studies of the atom, Niels Bohr received the Nobel Prize in physics in 1922.

HOLES OF GRAVITY AND BENT LIGHT

Albert Einstein had never considered his special theory of relativity to be finished, and in 1916 he published what he called the general theory of relativity, which rounded out his thoughts. It presented some ideas that were as astounding and dazzling as a science fiction story—such things as holes of gravity that would pull in anything that came near them, and curves in the emptiness of space that would make light bend!

It had been known for some time that the matter that makes up the universe has three dimensions, which are length, width, and thickness. But in his special theory of relativity, Einstein had suggested there was a fourth dimension—time. Nothing can exist in space without also existing in time, he pointed out. He maintained that all four dimensions were linked together, and implied that it was not correct to just speak of "space," but that people should speak of "space-time."

In his general theory of relativity, Einstein presented his ideas about what might be found in space-time. He suggested that gravity is actually caused by a "curvature of space," meaning that an object in space, such as a star, actually *bends* the space around it! This seems dreadfully hard to understand, for how can what seems to be mostly emptiness be bent? But this idea can actually be demonstrated by stretching a sheet of material, such as thin plastic, out flat to represent space. If a heavy object such as a baseball, representing a star or planet, is placed on the sheet, it will make a slight depression in the material under it. This depression represents the curvature of space. If a small marble is then tossed onto the sheet, it will roll in a curving path that will finally carry it into the depression around the ball—just as a smaller object in space, such as a meteoroid, is pulled toward a larger one, such as a planet.

The study of starlight during a solar eclipse proved Einstein's theory that gravity bends light.

Einstein's mathematics showed that even light is affected by gravity, and would be pulled into a curve if it passed a large object such as a star. And the mathematics suggested to some scientists that there must be "holes" of gravity in space—the remains of large stars that had collapsed and been pulled together until nothing was left of them but their gravity. The enormous gravity of such a hole would pull in anything that came near enough to it, even light. And because the light could not escape from it, it would not be visible. It would truly be a black hole.

Einstein's mathematics also indicated something else that was astonishing—that the universe was actually expanding, growing larger, because things in it, such as star clusters, are moving rapidly apart from one another. All this seemed like science fiction, and many scientists were doubtful of such incredible ideas. But then, in 1919, Einstein's statement that gravity bent light was found to be absolutely correct. A noted astronomer was able to measure starlight passing the sun during a full solar eclipse (when sunlight would not block out the starlight), and found that it did indeed bend. And a number of years later, astronomers also determined that the universe is expanding, as Einstein's mathematics had indicated.

Einstein became hailed as one of the greatest scientists and thinkers of all time. Our present understanding of the universe is based on his theory of relativity.

EINSTEIN'S BIGGEST MISTAKE

When Einstein saw that his mathematics for the general theory of relativity showed that the universe was expanding, he simply couldn't believe it. So he "fudged" the mathematics, and stuck in an equation that suggested the universe could never change.

Years later, when astronomers discovered that the universe was, indeed, expanding, Einstein lamented that changing his mathematics had been his "biggest mistake."

2

CHEMISTRY

Early chemists worked mainly with minerals and gases, which are inorganic (nonliving) substances, taken out of the earth or air. But in the early 1800s, more and more chemists began to experiment with substances based on carbon, an element that is present in all living things. Chemistry dealing with such substances is known as organic chemistry.

By the second half of the nineteenth century, organic chemistry had produced a number of useful new materials, such as vulcanized rubber, celluloid (a kind of plastic), and the explosive nitroglycerine, as well as artificial dyes and perfumes. This trend of looking to chemistry for new artificial and artificially produced materials led to some important finds in the first years of the twentieth century.

Throughout the nineteenth century, most chemists worked by themselves, in tiny "home" laboratories, and this was often still the situation in the beginning of the twentieth century. However, the tremendous financial success of artificial dyes, rubber, and other products created by chemistry led to the construction of large industrial laboratories, employing many chemists. Such laboratories were becoming common in Germany, the United States, and other industrialized nations as the twentieth century began.

THE NEW METAL

One of the great scientists of history was so poor that she was almost unable to afford to keep working on one of her most important discoveries.

When it was discovered in 1897 that the metal uranium gave off radiation, Marie Curie, a Polish woman married to a Frenchman, became one of the first scientists to study this strange occurrence. It was Marie Curie who found that another metal, thorium, also gave off radiation, and it was she

Marie and Pierre Curie began their study of radiation in 1897, one year after this photograph was taken.

who invented the term *radioactivity*, still in use today, to describe the radiating activity of the two metals. In 1898, she and her husband, Pierre, working together, discovered a totally new radioactive metal, unknown until then. Marie named it polonium, in honor of her native country. Shortly after that, they discovered still another new radioactive metal, which they named radium. All these discoveries had made Marie and Pierre Curie famous among scientists, but had not brought them any money. Pierre's job as a teacher at a small college barely provided enough for their needs.

So, as the nineteenth century drew to a close, the Curies found themselves with a problem. They knew that the new metal radium was generally present in tiny amounts in the kind of rock called pitchblende, but they had never actually removed any radium from pitchblende. They felt they really had to do this, because a lot of questions needed to be answered about radium. What did it weigh? What did it look like? What wonderful things might be learned by doing experiments with it? None of these questions could be answered until some actual pure radium was available. In order to finish their work, the Curies had to remove some radium from the pitchblende containing it.

But this would be a long and costly process. Marie and Pierre estimated that they would probably need at least 1 ton (0.9 metric ton) of pitchblende to get just a few ounces of radium, but pitchblende was expensive and they simply didn't have enough money. Would they be unable to finish their important scientific work just because they were poor?

Luck came to their aid. In Austria, there was a government-owned factory that dug up pitchblende by the hundreds of tons, removed a metal from it, then just threw it away. An Austrian scientist who was a friend of the Curies persuaded his government to give them a ton of the leftover pitchblende at no cost.

Working in a drafty, leaky shed as her laboratory, Marie went to work boiling down all the pitchblende into tiny amounts and separating out the material that gave off radiation. She soon found that one ton of pitchblende wouldn't be sufficient, and in order to obtain enough radium to be of any use, she actually had to boil down and separate out nearly eight tons (seven metric tons)! Finally, in 1902, after four years of work that was mostly sheer drudgery, she had a tiny amount of pure radium. It turned out to be a silvery white metal that glowed in the dark with a pale blue light.

It also turned out to be a very useful substance that has a number of scientific uses and is helpful in the treatment of cancer and some other diseases. In 1911, Marie Curie was awarded the Nobel Prize in chemistry for discovering polonium and radium and for isolating (separating) radium and studying it.

THE FIRST ARTIFICIAL PLASTIC

Leo Baekeland was born in Belgium, where he studied chemistry in college. Convinced that he could become wealthy by emigrating to America, he emigrated to America—and became wealthy, by inventing a photographic paper that made a great deal of money for him.

In the early years of the twentieth century, working in a laboratory he had built next to his home, Baekeland began trying to find an answer to a problem that had baffled chemists for years. When carbolic acid, which is a white, powdery substance made from coal tar, was mixed with formaldehyde, a liquid with a sharp, stinging odor, the result was a hard, brittle material. It was believed that if this substance could be dissolved into a liquid, it would make an excellent artificial shellac, much less expensive than the natural kind.

Baekeland was unable to find any way of dissolving the material. But it suddenly occurred to him that perhaps the hard material itself could be made useful. He began "cooking" quantities of it in a big iron pressure cooker in his laboratory, trying to turn it into a liquid that could be poured into molds and would then turn hard again. In 1907, he produced a material that was rock hard, almost unbreakable, could not be damaged by heat or chemicals, and weighed far less than most metals. It could be molded into any shape and dyed bright colors.

What Leo Baekeland had created was the first completely artificial plastic, a substance totally different from anything produced by nature. He named it Bakelite.

Baekeland's discovery changed the world as greatly as Marconi's invention of radio or the Wright brothers' invention of the airplane. It was the beginning of the age of plastics. Today, just about anything that was

Leo Baekeland created an entirely new substance, one not found in nature.

Plastic has become a common part of everyday life in the latter part of the twentieth century.

once made of wood, metal, ivory, or bone can be made out of an artificial plastic, of which Bakelite was the first.

A Process for Unlimited Plant Food

Nitrogen is a colorless, odorless, tasteless gas that makes up more than three-fourths of the world's air. It is also mixed into several different kinds of chemical compounds (substances) that are found in the soil as liquids. In 1840, a French chemist discovered that plants are able to tap into these compounds with their roots and take the nitrogen out of them. In time, scientists understood that plants use nitrogen as food. When they get enough of it, they grow bigger and are more healthy than they are if they lack nitrogen. It became obvious that farmers could grow better crops if they put nitrogen compounds into the soil as fertilizer.

But most of the nitrogen is in the air, and nitrogen compounds in the ground are not very plentiful. At the beginning of the twentieth century, there simply was not enough nitrogen fertilizer available to grow all the food needed for the world's increasing population.

In 1909, a German chemist named Fritz Haber found an answer for this problem. One of the best sources for nitrogen fertilizer is a gas called ammonia, which is formed of one part nitrogen and three parts hydrogen, another gas found mainly in the ground. Haber discovered how to combine nitrogen from the air with hydrogen from the ground—very inexpensive materials—to produce ammonia artificially. Once the ammonia was being manufactured in large quantities, it could easily be turned into compounds such as one called ammonium nitrate, which is an excellent fertilizer because plants can easily get the nitrogen out of it.

Haber sold his method of making ammonia to a big German chemical firm known as BASF Company. In 1913, a BASF chemist, Karl Bosch, supervised the building of a factory that could manufacture enormous amounts of ammonia and then turn it into nitrogen compounds for fertilizer and other things. The factory's method for producing ammonia became known as the Haber process. This same process, with some improvements, is still used throughout the world, after more than eighty years, to produce fertilizer. Fritz Haber's discovery of how to make ammonia artificially was a tremendous aid to world agriculture, and he was awarded the Nobel Prize in chemistry in 1918. For his part in developing Haber's discovery into an industrial process, Karl Bosch received the Nobel Prize in 1931.

THE BIRTH OF A GREAT INDUSTRY

As the twentieth century began, people in many places were lighting their homes with lamps that burned a liquid called kerosene. Kerosene was produced by heating petroleum, or crude oil, in large open containers. This was known as refining, and the industrial plants where it was done were called refineries. When the kerosene was produced, there was always a small amount of another substance left, which was known as stove naphtha, because it could be used as fuel for specially made cookstoves. But most of it was just thrown away.

At this time, most wealthy people had horses and carriages to take them places. Less well-off people took streetcars (trolley cars) or just walked when they needed to go short distances, and rode in trains when they had to go far. But the new invention, the automobile, also known as the horseless carriage, was becoming more and more popular. Many of these vehicles were powered by engines that burned stove naphtha for fuel. So, as more and more autos were built and sold, more and more of the special fuel was needed. However, there simply wasn't enough of it produced when petroleum was refined into kerosene, and no one knew of a way to get more of it out of petroleum.

Then, in 1911, William Burton, an American chemist who was a refinery superintendent with Standard Oil Company, conducted a dangerous experiment. He heated some petroleum in a closed container. There could have been an explosion, but fortunately, there wasn't. Instead, many of the large molecules (clusters of atoms) that generally formed kerosene were literally cracked apart by the pressure, and formed the substance called stove naphtha.

This process became known as cracking, and the substance that it produced soon was named gasoline. Through the cracking process, it became possible for refineries to produce about twice as much gasoline (stove naphtha) as they had before. With gasoline more plentiful, the future of automobiles was assured, and with the increase in automobiles, the production of gasoline became a gigantic, tremendously important industry.

3

ASTRONOMY

Up until the middle of the nineteenth century, astronomers had nothing much more than their eyes, telescopes, and mathematics to help them learn about objects in space. Based upon what they could see and estimate, they believed for the most part that the Milky Way galaxy (the grouping of hundreds of billions of stars in which our solar system is located) was the entire universe. They believed that all stars had about the same brightness, which meant that the dimmest stars were simply those that were farthest away, while the brightest were the closest. And they believed that it would never be possible to learn what stars were composed of.

But near the middle of the nineteenth century, there were two major inventions that changed all this. One was the invention of photography. It became possible to take pictures through telescopes of regions of space, and to compare and study them. The other invention was a machine called a spectrometer, which could spread out light, including the light given off by a star, showing it as a spectrum of colors from blue to green to yellow to orange to red. Because every chemical substance emits a different color spectrum when heated, it was possible to identify chemicals by their spectrums. And so it also became possible to find out what chemicals were in every star—what stars were composed of.

By the beginning of the twentieth century, there was an enormous amount of information available from these sources, and there were a number of astronomers making use of it. Because these people used devices and methods much like those used by physicists, they became known as astrophysicists, meaning "star physicists." In the early years of the twentieth century, some of them made discoveries that led to incredible leaps of knowledge about space and our place in it.

A Way to Measure the Universe

In the year 1596, a German astronomer named David Fabricius became aware that he had found a star that seemed to change in brightness over a period of time. It would be bright for a while, then would grow dim, then would turn bright again. Fabricius had discovered the first of what are now called variable (changing) stars.

By the beginning of the twentieth century, 113 of these odd stars had been discovered. There were several kinds of them. Some grew bright very suddenly, stayed that way for a time, then grew dim again. These are known as novas. Another kind seemed to pulse; they grew bright, then dim, then bright, then dim. These were named Cepheid (SEE-fee-id) variables, because the first of them was discovered in the constellation called Cepheus.

In 1911, Henrietta S. Leavitt, an American astronomer at the Harvard College Observatory, began the task of examining photographs of different

Henrietta S. Leavitt's study of variable stars led to the discovery of a method for measuring distances to the stars.

regions of space, looking for variable stars. The brighter a star is, the larger a spot it makes on a photo, so to look for variables, Leavitt had to examine scores of photographs of the same region, looking at every spot to see if it got bigger or smaller from one photo to the next. This took hundreds of painstaking hours!

Leavitt did find some variable stars, but what was far more important was something she noticed about Cepheid variables. In 1912, she reported that Cepheids that took a longer period of time to go from bright to dim and back to bright again were generally far brighter than those with short periods. The full importance of this was not obvious at first, but it was really a major discovery. It meant that the period of a Cepheid's change could be accurately measured, and its luminosity, or brightness, could be determined exactly. This eventually led to a way of measuring enormous distances to stars and other objects very far from earth, for if a star's luminosity can be determined, its distance from earth can be estimated by mathematics. Leavitt's long hours of tedious work had produced a very valuable tool that enabled astronomers to discover that there are other galaxies, far beyond the galaxy our world is in, and that the universe is far bigger than was ever imagined at the beginning of the twentieth century. It was a way of measuring the universe!

THE CHARACTERISTICS OF STARS

When you look up at the stars in a night sky, they all seem to be tiny points of white light. But since the invention of the telescope, in the 1600s, astronomers have known that stars have different colors. There are red, blue, green, orange, yellow, and even brownish stars, as well as white ones.

For a long time, it was generally believed that there was no particular reason why stars have different colors—that it was just pure chance. But late in the nineteenth century, astronomers realized that there was a very good reason for this. A star's color depended quite simply upon how hot it was. A piece of metal can be heated until it glows a dazzling white, but as it cools, its color will change, from white to yellow to orange to red. And so it is with stars. For the most part, the hottest stars are blue; the next hottest are bluish white; then come white, yellow, orange, and red, the coolest—if a temperature of around 5,500°F (3,038°C) can be thought of as cool!

Once this was known, it suddenly seemed to some astronomers that if there was a reason for a star's color, there might be reasons for other characteristics of stars, too. Perhaps it wasn't all just a matter of chance. And early in the twentieth century, two astronomers thousands of miles apart found this was indeed true. Unknown to each other, Ejnar Hertzsprung of Denmark and Henry Norris Russell, an American, both had the idea of matching the colors of stars against their brightness and making a graph, or chart, of what this showed. What both Hertzsprung and Russell found was that stars of the same color all had about the same brightness. Thus, three of a star's characteristics—color, hotness, and brightness—were dependent upon one another.

When Hertzsprung's and Russell's findings became known, around 1913, the charts the two men had each worked out were combined into what was called the Hertzsprung-Russell diagram. On this chart, star colors are shown by vertical bars of blue, blue-white, white, yellow, orange, and red, and brightness is shown by a row of numbers running down alongside the first color bar. When the color and brightness of a star were determined, the star was put onto the chart, represented by a dot located on the proper color and in line with the correct brightness number. It was found that most stars fit into a diagonal line stretching from the upper left (bluest and brightest) to the lower right (reddest and least bright). It turned out that most stars that fit into this diagonal path are all about the same size, which is medium to small, as stars go. The stars fitting onto the diagonal are known as main sequence stars, and earth's sun is a main sequence star that appears almost exactly in the middle of the chart, a little more than halfway down. It is a small-sized, medium bright star, described as a yellow dwarf.

The Hertzsprung-Russell diagram identifies other kinds of stars besides those on the main sequence. There are yellow and red giant stars that are considerably bigger and brighter than our sun, and blue, white, and red supergiants that are titanically bigger. There are also white dwarf stars, considerably smaller and dimmer than the sun.

The Hertzsprung-Russell diagram also helps determine the ages of stars. From a star's color, temperature, size, and mass (the amount of gas forming it), astronomers can determine how much of its gas a star has burned, and that tells how long it has been glowing—how old it is. The fiercely bright blue and blue-white stars of average size are young, in some cases no more than a hundred million years old. Our little yellow sun is "middle-aged." It has been glowing for about five billion years and has about five billion more to go. Red stars are old, with most of their fuel used up. When our sun has used up most of its fuel, it will swell up and become a "cool" red giant. Then it will no longer be a main sequence star.

The work of Ejnar Hertzsprung and Henry Russell gave astronomers a major tool for classifying stars and determining their ages. And in time, this led to the great discovery of the age of the universe itself.

EVIDENCE OF AN EXPANDING UNIVERSE

For about 200 years before the start of the twentieth century, astronomers had been able to see certain fuzzy "blobs" out in space that did not seem to be stars. They were called nebulae, from the Latin word for *mist*. By the beginning of the twentieth century, there were two ideas about what these misty objects might be. One was that they were whirlpools of gas that were slowly being pulled together by gravity and forming into new stars. Astronomers who backed this idea felt that nebulae were probably fairly small and that, of course, they were all inside the Milky Way (where our solar system is) because the Milky Way was generally thought to be the entire universe. The other idea was that the Milky Way was not the entire universe, but was merely a galaxy, and the nebulae were actually other galaxies, far away across the gulfs of space.

In 1912, an American astronomer named Vesto Slipher began using a spectroscope to study a number of nebulae in an attempt to determine once and for all what they were. It had been found that a spectroscope (a spectrometer attached to a telescope) could be used to detect the motion of stars. Stars that were moving toward earth showed more high-frequency blue light on a spectroscope, while those moving away from earth showed more low-frequency red.

Slipher expected to find only some slow, rotating motion that could indicate the nebulae were indeed forming into stars. Instead, he found rapid, headlong movement. By 1917, he had checked twenty-five nebulae, and twenty-one showed color at the red end of the spectrum. This meant they

A false-color image of a spiral galaxy, NGC 1232

were all moving away from earth, which was quite surprising. Furthermore, they were all moving very fast, much faster than stars.

Slipher announced his findings in 1917. Neither he nor anyone else knew it, but he was actually the first person to find evidence that the universe is expanding. It would not be until 1924 that astronomers would know for sure that the nebulae known as spiral nebulae, because of their shape, are actually galaxies that are enormous distances away from the Milky Way galaxy. And it would not be until 1929 that astronomers would understand that the galaxies are all rushing away from one another, as the universe slowly spreads apart. So no one in 1917 had any idea of what Slipher's findings meant. But today, they are regarded as a major discovery.

4

BIOLOGY

Biology is the science that studies how living things are constructed, and how they survive, live together, and stay healthy. Medical science is, of course, a branch of biology.

In the nineteenth century, biology consisted mainly of studying nature, and people who did so were known as naturalists. They were mainly concerned with learning how animals lived and in finding new kinds of animals and plants. But out of the studies of animals, plants, and medicine came several extremely important discoveries.

One, by a naturalist, was the discovery that living things slowly change over great periods of time, producing new species, or kinds, of animals and plants. A second discovery, actually made by a number of both naturalists and doctors, was that cells—microscopic blobs of living jellylike substance—form the bodies of all living things and are literally the building blocks of life. A third discovery, made by a doctor and a chemist, was that some diseases are caused by bacteria (germs). A fourth discovery, made by a botanist (plant scientist), was that characteristics of plants and animals, such as size and color, are passed along from parents to young from a special source that is within every living thing.

These discoveries, one of which was completely ignored during the nineteenth century, were of great significance in the early years of the twentieth century. They led to advances that are of major importance today.

THE BIRTH OF GENETICS

In the 1800s, a Czech priest and teacher named Gregor Mendel spent years of his life learning some remarkable things about living creatures. When he died, the records of his discoveries were stored away and forgotten. In the first year of the twentieth century, they were rediscovered through an amazing coincidence and became the foundation of an entire new field of science that is of tremendous importance.

Father Gregor Mendel lived at a monastery in the city of Brno, in what is now the Czech Republic. In 1856, he began to experiment with pea plants growing in the monastery garden. He was interested in trying to find out how certain characteristics of the plants, such as size, shape of the seeds, and color of the flowers, were passed along from one generation to another. He began a program of breeding and crossbreeding plants for seven years, deliberately pollinating certain plants with the pollen of others instead of letting it happen naturally. He carefully recorded every characteristic of every plant in each generation.

Mendel learned that when plants with different characteristics were crossed, they produced seeds from which grew new plants that contained one or the other of the different characteristics, and that this could be accurately predicted by mathematics. From this, he decided that every living thing must have within itself some source for all its characteristics, a source that could be passed along to its descendants.

Mendel reported his findings to a number of scientific organizations, but there was absolutely no interest in them. It seemed as if most scientists felt this knowledge was of no use and no significance. Gregor Mendel died in 1884, with his name and his work completely unknown to the world of science.

The 1900s dawned and the amazing coincidence occurred. Three men, hundreds of miles apart from one another, began to experiment along the same lines Mendel had, although they didn't even know that he had ever existed. These men were biologists Hugo de Vries of the Netherlands, Carl Correns of Germany, and Erich von Seysenegg of Austria. At about the same time, each man, seeking help in his work, searched through scientific records to see if anyone else had ever done any experiments or conducted any studies of how characteristics were passed along from one generation to the next. All three men came across the records of Gregor Mendel's work.

When de Vries, Correns, and von Seysenegg published descriptions of their own work, they all included information about Mendel and his discoveries. Thus, Mendel's work became known, and now its importance was understood. The source for characteristics that Mendel had discovered became known as genes, from a Greek word meaning "breed," or "kind." That word became the basis for the name of an entire new science that has become one of the most important sciences of the twentieth century—genetics. By means of what is known as genetic engineering, scientists are becoming able to alter genes and thereby eliminate diseases and disorders in people, and to cause various kinds of changes in living things.

DIFFERENCES IN BLOOD

In the late 1600s, doctors began to realize that an injured person in danger of dying from loss of blood could be saved by having the blood replaced with blood from someone else. Thus, the idea of blood transfusion—a possible way of saving many lives—was born.

But when doctors began attempting blood transfusions, they found that often the person receiving the new blood died. No one could understand why. It seemed as if all human blood were the same, so why would one person's blood cause the death of another? Doctors didn't know, but they soon stopped trying to do blood transfusions.

However, doctors were still interested in finding out everything they could about blood, and continued to examine it, test it, and experiment with it. By the beginning of the twentieth century, microscopes had become sufficiently powerful and well constructed so that a really good examination of blood was possible. And in 1900, an Austrian doctor named Karl Landsteiner made a very important observation with his microscope.

Landsteiner found that if red blood cells of an animal were mixed with serum (the liquid part)

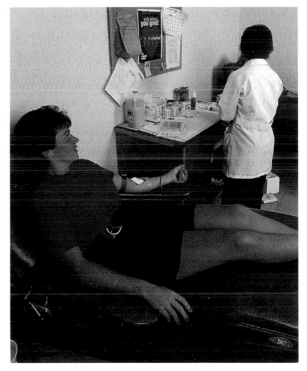

Blood donations are identified by type, making safe transfusions possible.

disease—a species known as *Aedes aegypti*. Reed and the other doctors decided they must find out for sure if Finlay was right.

There was only one way to do this. They allowed *Aedes* mosquitoes to bite some yellow fever patients so that the mosquitoes would become carriers of the disease. The insects were quickly captured in test tubes, and then two of the doctors deliberately allowed themselves to be bitten. One did not get the disease; the other, Dr. James Carroll, came down with a severe case, but recovered. However, one of the other men, Dr. Jesse Lazear, was accidentally bitten, got the disease, and died.

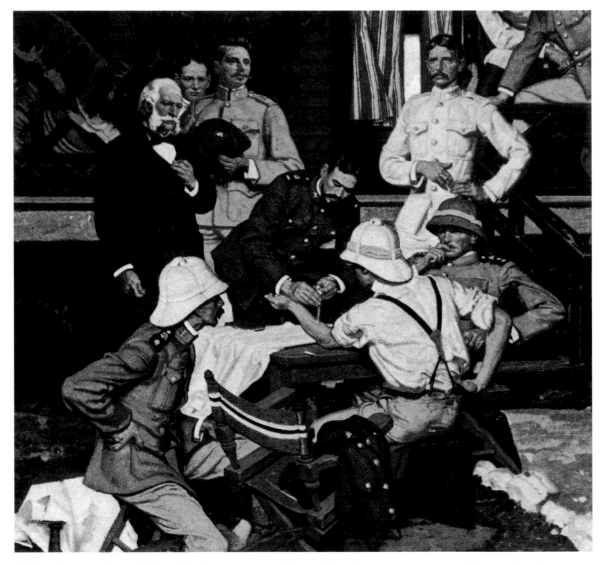

This painting shows Walter Reed, center, working with volunteers as part of his study of yellow fever.

This was strong evidence, but Major Reed had to be absolutely sure that it was indeed the mosquitoes that caused yellow fever and not simply germs in the air, as many doctors believed. He asked for volunteers among the American soldiers. Seven men volunteered to let themselves be bitten by disease-carrying mosquitoes. A number of others agreed to stay for twenty days in a screened hut (so that mosquitoes could not get in) that contained bedding and clothing of yellow fever patients. If germs carried the disease, there would certainly be germs in the bedding and clothing, and the volunteers would be infected.

None of the men who had been in the hut came down with yellow fever. Five of the seven who had been bitten by mosquitoes did. This was the final proof. In 1902, Major Reed was able to report positively that yellow fever was caused by the *Aedes aegypti* mosquito, which transmitted either a bacteria or a virus to the people it bit.

The work of Major Walter Reed's group is regarded as one of the great achievements of medical science. Once it was known for sure how yellow fever was caused, it was possible to take preventive measures. This was done by attacking the mosquito larvae (young). Swamps in which mosquitoes laid their eggs were drained, pools of stagnant water were eliminated, and ponds were covered with a film of oil, killing the larvae when they hatched. Although the disease still could not be totally prevented, it was brought under greater control. As a result, it became possible to build the Panama Canal in an area where yellow fever had once raged. Construction of the canal began in 1903.

DISCOVERING A VITAL INGREDIENT

In the language of the Sinhalese people of Southeast Asia, the word *beriberi* means "I cannot." This word is used as the name for a dreadful disease that was once common throughout Southeast Asia, for it made people so sick that they literally could not do anything. It caused paralysis (inability to move) and great pain. Victims of beriberi often died of heart failure.

Around 1900, a Dutch army doctor named Christiaan Eijkman was stationed in Indonesia, which was then a Dutch colony. Like most doctors, Eijkman felt sure that beriberi was caused by a germ. But then, something rather odd happened, and led him to a startling discovery. A small flock of

Because of his knowledge of chemistry, Ehrlich believed that medicines made from chemicals could be used to treat disease. With the assistance of a group of workers at the institute, he began to search for what he called a magic bullet—a chemical substance that could be injected into a sick person's body and would head right for the disease bacteria and destroy them. He prepared hundreds of chemical combinations and tested them on animals that had been infected with various diseases.

Ehrlich was not the only researcher looking for cures through chemistry. Scientists in many parts of the world were trying out chemical compounds, and one, made from the metal arsenic, showed some promise. Ehrlich began to use an arsenic compound called atoxyl as the basis for some of the medicines he tested on animals.

One of the worst diseases in the world at this time was syphilis. It was a brutal disease that slowly spread through a person's body, eventually causing paralysis, blindness, insanity, and death. There was very little that could be done for it, but in 1905 a German doctor named Fritz Schaudin had discovered the cause of it—bacteria that resembled twisted rods. At Ehrlich's orders, his assistants began testing arsenic compounds on rabbits that had been infected with syphilis, and by 1909 they had tried more than 600. In the spring of 1909, a compound known as Number 606 was tried—and it worked.

Ehrlich announced his discovery of a successful treatment for syphilis in 1910. The news caused rejoicing throughout the world. Ehrlich had already been awarded a Nobel Prize in physiology or medicine in 1908, shared with another scientist, for work on studying how the human body fights off disease. Under the rules, he could not be given another. But he was showered with honors.

Paul Ehrlich invented the term *chemotherapy* for the use of chemicals to treat disease. His discovery of Number 606 started the whole field of chemotherapy—a field that is an important part of medicine today.

Red-Eyed Fruit Flies

The answer to a major question about heredity came from humble red-eyed fruit flies. In order to learn more about heredity, scientists had to do as Gregor Mendel had done and study generations—the time in which a creature is born, grows to be an adult, and creates offspring, or young ones. Of

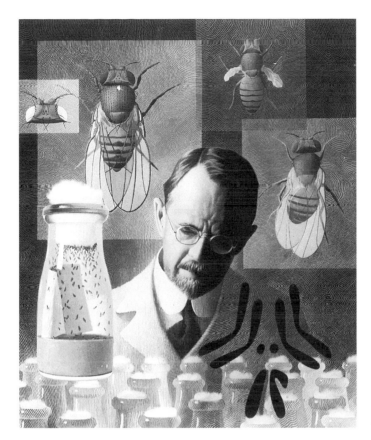

*Thomas Hunt Morgan's fruit-fly
research spanned several decades.*

course, many generations had to be studied in order to watch characteristics
being passed along. This meant that scientists couldn't study human generations, because those take about twenty years. Even generations of animals
such as dogs or cats were far too long. So when a biology professor named
Thomas Hunt Morgan began to study heredity in 1907, he picked red-eyed
fruit fly generations to watch. Red-eyed fruit flies have very short lives and
quick generations of only a few days, so Morgan could observe many, many
generations in just a few months.

Morgan and others were trying to find the answer to the question, Where
are the characteristics that parents pass along to their young kept? What part
of a person's body, or a plant's form, contains the genes that tell what color a
child's eyes will be, or how long a flower's stem will become? A number of
biologists thought the answer might lie in things called chromosomes.

Chromosomes were discovered in 1888. They are stringlike objects in
the nucleus, or center, of every plant and animal cell. A human cell nucleus
has forty-six chromosomes. In 1891, an American biologist found a particular

chromosome, which he called X, that was transmitted from parent to off-spring.

Morgan and his assistants concentrated on red-eyed fruit fly chromosomes. In 1910, they found that certain characteristics, such as eye color, were definitely caused by the X chromosome. When a mutant white-eyed male fly appeared in a jar full of normal red-eyes, the next generation had a number of white-eyed males. The first white-eye had passed his eye color along to some of his young by means of his X chromosome.

Examining chromosomes under the microscope, Morgan and his helpers found that they were "banded," like a string painted with stripes at regular intervals. In 1911, Morgan announced that these bands were nothing less than the genes, the sources of a creature's characteristics. Each gene carries a different "message," which in the case of humans determines hair color, eye color, body size, et cetera. Thus, with the help of red-eyed fruit flies, Thomas Hunt Morgan had solved the riddle of where characteristics come from. In 1933, Morgan was awarded the Nobel Prize for his studies of the function of chromosomes in heredity.

5

GEOLOGY

Geology is the study of our world. Geologists are scientists who investigate how the earth was formed, how it has changed over millions of years, and what has caused those changes. A special branch of geology called paleontology, the study of prehistoric life, seeks to find out what living things were like during all the hundreds of millions of years of earth's past.

Up until the last years of the 1700s, it was generally believed that the world was only about 6,000 years old and had never been any different from the way it was in the eighteenth century. The idea that there might have been different seas and mountain ranges at one time, to say nothing of different kinds of plants and animals from those alive in the 1700s, was simply not even considered by most people.

Then, in the early 1800s, there was a sudden swirl of change. An idea called uniformitarianism began to take hold. This was the idea that the surface of the earth is slowly but constantly changing, due to the action of wind, rain, snow, floods, earthquakes, and volcanoes, over a period of many years. The discovery of fossil bones of unknown animals, such as dinosaurs, provided evidence that there had once been animals very different from those currently living. These things became the foundation of geology.

By the beginning of the twentieth century, geologists were studying all the causes that had changed the earth, and paleontologists were seeking out remains of prehistoric creatures. Exciting discoveries about prehistoric life, and an astonishing idea about how the world changes, marked the first two decades of the century.

THE BEAST ON THE RIVERBANK

On an August day in 1900, a Russian man by the name of Semen Tarabykin was plodding along the bank of the Berezovka River, in Siberia. With him was his dog. They were hunting, and had picked up the trail of an elk. The two had hunted together often, but they were about to make an amazing discovery.

Suddenly, the dog paused, its nose quivering at a strange scent. It darted off at top speed, and breaking into a trot, Tarabykin followed. He caught up with the dog some distance away. It was standing on the riverbank, peering down at something. Joining it, Tarabykin was astounded to see a huge motionless shape, half buried in the soil of the riverbank—a bulky, red-furred animal with curling tusks.

It is thousands of miles from the Berezovka River to any of the big cities of western Russia, and in 1900 there were no airplanes or automobiles, no radio, and no long-distance telephone lines. It took nearly a year for news of Tarabykin's discovery to reach the Russian Academy of Sciences in the city of Saint Petersburg. From the description of the beast Tarabykin had found, Russian paleontologists knew that it could only be a prehistoric woolly mammoth—an elephantlike creature whose kind had become extinct some 10,000 years earlier. Many skeletons of mammoths had been found, but it was clear that what Tarabykin had discovered was the entire body of a mammoth that had somehow been preserved, intact, for thousands of years. It would be an incredible treasure trove of information!

A team of paleontologists set out almost at once, but it was nearly four months more before they reached the carcass. By now, the exposed part of

This painting shows an artist's concept of a prehistoric woolly mammoth, like the one discovered on the bank of the Berezovka River.

the animal had begun to rot, and parts of it had been eaten by wolves and other animals. Even so, there was enough of it left to answer a score of questions about how these giant furred animals had looked and lived when herds of them were still roaming the northern parts of the earth.

The scientists went to work to dig the body out of the frozen ground. It was carefully skinned, then it was cut apart and each part was thoroughly examined. It is known that prehistoric people ate the meat of mammoths, and the scientists were tempted to cook some up and try it, but they were fearful of becoming ill. However, they tried out some cooked mammoth meat on their sled dogs. The animals ate it up gladly, and suffered no ill effects.

The mammoth was a young male. The scientists found that beneath its shaggy red hair it was covered with a soft, yellowish, woolly fur. This would have kept it warm even in the fiercest cold of the Ice Age, during which mammoths lived. Examining its stomach, the scientists were delighted to find remains of the food the animal had eaten on the very day it died—buttercups. This was the kind of information that all the fossil skeletons in the world could never have provided!

The men were even able to determine how the animal had died. It had been foraging on a part of the riverbank that had suddenly collapsed under its weight, and it had fallen 20 feet (6 meters) into shallow water. It had landed in a sitting position, with such force that its right hip and foreleg were broken. An avalanche of icy mud from the riverbank had poured down with the creature, totally burying it, and it had quickly suffocated.

Of course, this was the time of the Ice Age, and the dirt covering the mammoth had quickly frozen hard, also freezing the mammoth's body. For years, eroded by icy rains and wind, more of the riverbank had slid down to pile atop the mound covering the beast. Thus, even when the Ice Age ended, the mammoth was kept frozen stone hard and protected for some 40,000 years, for in cold Siberia, the ground never thaws more than a few inches deep.

But eventually, over many centuries, erosion wore away the frozen earth covering the mammoth, bringing the creature's body closer to the surface. In the spring of 1900, torrents of rain fell, washing away the last of the icy earth on the mammoth's head and shoulders, leaving it visible for Tarabykin to find by pure luck.

Since that time, frozen remains of about fifty other mammoths have been found in Siberia and Alaska. But the Berezovka mammoth was the first to give us a really good picture of what these extinct beasts were like in life. It ranks as one of the great scientific discoveries of the twentieth century.

The Finding of the "King"

As a boy, Barnum Brown found it fun to search for and collect fossils in the part of Kansas where he grew up. As a man, he became one of the most renowned dinosaur fossil collectors in America, and discovered one of the most famous of all dinosaurs.

In the summer of 1902, Brown went into the rough "badlands" country of Montana. It was an area that had never been looked over by any paleontologist, but Brown had learned that cowboys and sheepherders who worked in

Barnum Brown with the skeleton of an Allosaurus. *Brown's major dinosaur discovery introduced* Tyrannosaurus rex *to the world.*

Tyrannosaurus rex, *the "Tyrant reptile king"!*

the region had reported finding strange bones. It was country that contained rock formations from what is known as the Cretaceous period of prehistory, which lasted from 144 million to 65 million years ago. This was the last period of the Mesozoic age—the Age of Dinosaurs—and the animals that had lived at that time were not as well known in 1902 as those of earlier periods.

Brown set up camp in a narrow valley through which ran a small creek. A few days later, he made what would turn out to be a sensational discovery. In the sandstone bank of the creek, he found some brownish bones. He could not do any actual digging, but he carefully noted the location.

In 1905, Brown returned with his digging crew. They began to take the bones of what seemed to be the skeleton of a very large two-legged dinosaur from the riverbank. In time, it could be seen that what Barnum Brown had found was the back half—hips, legs, and tail—of the largest flesh-eating dinosaur that had ever been discovered. In life it would have been a good 40 feet (12 meters) long and 19 feet (5.8 meters) high. A man 6 feet (1.8 meters) tall would have reached only to its knee. The sharp, curved claws on its feet indicated that it was a predator (hunter) and its size made it the biggest flesh-eating land animal that was known. It would have been the king of beasts in its world! So it was named *Tyrannosaurus rex*, meaning "Tyrant reptile king."

Yes, the dinosaur Barnum Brown discovered in 1902 was *Tyrannosaurus*, which is now one of the most "popular" dinosaurs, known throughout the world. Brown dug up a great many other dinosaur skeletons, but his 1902 discovery that introduced *Tyrannosaurus* to the world was a milestone in paleontology.

THE AGE OF ROCKS

By the beginning of the twentieth century, geologists knew that the earth must be far more than 6,000 years old, as had been believed only 100 years earlier. But they had no idea how old earth actually was, and so they had no way of knowing when all the different kinds of prehistoric creatures had lived. The paleontologist who gave *Tyrannosaurus* its name thought that the huge flesh eater had lived "about a million years ago." (Actually, it was 70 million years ago.) Geologists in general thought that the earth was probably about 100 million years old. (In fact, it's about 4.5 billion.) There seemed to be no way geologists could ever figure out the exact age of the earth. After all, how could such a thing be done? How could you trace back through the passage of time?

Then, suddenly, there *was* a way. It came from the science of physics, and was discovered by the brilliant physicist Ernest Rutherford, who had solved the mystery of radioactivity. He revealed it one day in 1905. A professor of geology at McGill University, in Montreal, Canada, was walking across the campus when he saw Rutherford, a professor of physics at the university, coming toward him. Rutherford was holding something in his hand. In his loud, booming voice, he asked the geologist how old the earth was. The geology teacher explained that the exact age was not really known, but most geologists thought it must be about 100 million years old.

Rutherford showed what he was holding. It was a lump of black rock of the kind called pitchblende, which nearly always contains some of the radioactive metal radium. Rutherford boomed that he did not know the age of the world either, but he definitely knew the age of the piece of pitchblende. It was, he stated, 700 million years old!

Rutherford was not joking. His work on discovering the cause of radioactivity had led to an interesting side discovery and a marvelous idea. He had found that radioactive elements such as radium had what he called a half-life. This meant that the amount of the element and the amount of the radioactivity it gave off were reduced exactly by half over a certain period of time, until finally, all the radioactive particles were gone from the atoms of the element, and the element had become something else. In the case of radium, this half-life cycle occurred every 1,620 years, continuing for hundreds of millions of years.

But many particles given off remained in the pitchblende in the form of a gas called helium. Rutherford realized that by measuring the amount of helium and the amount of radium left in a piece of pitchblende, which can be done chemically, it would be possible to calculate when the half-life process had begun, at the moment the rock was formed. That, of course, would give the age of the rock.

Rutherford had seen that this would provide a way for geologists to determine the age of earth's layers of rock by measuring the amount of radioactive decay, or loss, that had taken place in radioactive elements within them. In 1907, American chemist Bertram Boltwood developed a method of establishing the age of rocks by measuring the decay of uranium into lead, and other methods were also soon developed. Geology had been given an incredible new tool!

DINOSAUR SKIN

One of the major discoveries about dinosaurs was made by four paleontologists who happened to be a father and his three sons.

In the summer of 1908, Charles Sternberg and his grown sons, George, Charles Jr., and Levi, were digging for fossils in Wyoming when they began to run short of food. Charles and Charles Jr. took the horse-drawn wagon to the nearest town for more supplies. While they were gone, George and Levi continued to chip away at the skeleton of an *Anatosaurus*—a duck-billed dinosaur—that the four men had found embedded in the side of a sandstone cliff.

The Sternbergs had uncovered the skeleton down to the breastbone, and it seemed quite ordinary. A number of *Anatosaurus* skeletons had already been found by paleontologists, so the two brothers weren't much excited by what they were doing. But when George lifted a large piece of rock off the *Anatosaurus*'s chest, the two men almost whooped with excitement. For the dinosaur's ribs were covered with petrified skin!

By the time their father and brother got back, George and Levi had uncovered the entire skeleton. It was lying on its back, stretched out full length with its head pointing straight up and one of its forelegs lifted as if it were reaching upward. And its bones were covered with patches of skin that had turned to stone as the bones had.

What had probably caused this to happen was that, some seventy million years ago, the *Anatosaurus* had been wandering through a desert area and had stepped into a patch of loose sand covering a deep gully. It had fallen in and quickly smothered to death, desperately stretching its head to reach air and pawing with its front legs to try to climb out of the loose sand all around it. After the animal had died, the dry, hot sand had sucked all the moisture out of its body, mummifying it so that the skin was stretched tight over the bones. Over millions of years, fossilization took place as bits of mineral replaced skin and bone, producing a stone copy of the *Anatosaurus*'s body.

Finding this skeleton was a tremendous discovery, because it answered a question that paleontologists had been wondering about for a good sixty years—what had a dinosaur's skin looked like? The petrified skin of the *Anatosaurus* revealed that when the animal was alive, its skin must have been much like that of a present-day lizard known as a Gila monster. It was thick and leathery and covered with little knobs and bumps. Some of these were arranged in small clusters, and they may have been a different color from the rest of the skin, forming spots of color all over the dinosaur's body.

The mummified skeleton revealed other things, as well. The skin on the handlike feet of the *Anatosaurus*'s front legs had been preserved and showed that the animal had webs between its toes. There was also a ruffle of thick skin that had been preserved running down the creature's back to the end of its tail. All this gave paleontologists a marvelous picture of what the

Anatosaurus had looked like alive, and gave them confidence that all dinosaurs must have had similar skin, much like that of present-day reptiles. The Sternbergs' wonderful discovery added a great deal to our knowledge of dinosaurs.

CREATURES OF AN ANCIENT SEA

In the early 1900s, Charles Walcott, a well-known American paleontologist, was in charge of the huge Smithsonian Institution. This was mainly a desk job, involving lots of paperwork, planning, and overseeing of things. But what Walcott really liked to do most was search for fossils out in the wilderness. That's what he generally spent his vacations doing. And it was on one such vacation, in the mountains of western Canada in 1909, that he made an unusual discovery. It was simply a huge slab of the kind of rock called shale, about as long as a city block and 10 feet (3 meters) thick. But many paleontologists now feel that this piece of rock was the most important discovery in the entire history of paleontology!

The reason for this is that the rock, which Walcott named the Burgess

Shale, contains the fossil remains of about 35,000 sea creatures that lived some 540 million years ago. This was a time before there was any life on land, and all the world's living things, plants and animals, were in the sea. The animals of that time were nearly all soft-bodied creatures, like worms or insects, and such creatures usually don't become very good fossils—there's generally nothing left of them but an impression of their top and bottom sides. However, the creatures of the Burgess Shale are so remarkably well preserved, with even their mouths and stomachs intact, that scientists can actually tell what some of them ate. Thus, the Burgess Shale gives us a wonderful picture of what life was like on a sandy sea bottom 540 million years ago.

But there is something even more remarkable about the Burgess Shale. It was formed during what is known as the Cambrian period, which lasted from about 505 million to 90 million years ago. At the beginning of the Cambrian period, there occurred what is known as the Cambrian Explosion—a literal explosion of life. While there are very, very few fossils of animals or plants dating from before the Cambrian period, an enormous amount seem to suddenly appear in rocks dating from after the Cambrian period began. Furthermore, many of the fossils are of brand-new creatures that didn't seem to exist before the Cambrian period, and that don't exist now. The Cambrian seas were swarming with more different kinds of living things than there are in the ocean today! It is very much as if something "spe-

cial" happened at the beginning of the Cambrian period, which perhaps caused a spurt in evolution and made many new kinds of creatures appear. The Burgess Shale has given us the best information we have about those creatures.

A number of the Burgess Shale creatures are completely different from any kind of animal living today. Some are so different that scientists aren't even sure what group of animals they belong to. None of

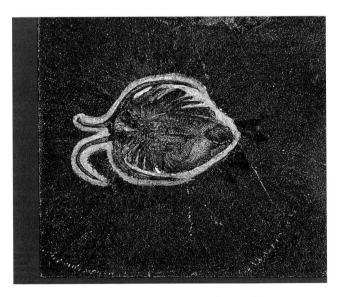

The fossil of a trilobite, preserved in the Burgess Shale.

them were very big—they range from a few inches to about 1 foot (30 centimeters) long—but nevertheless, they certainly fit the role of prehistoric "monsters"! One of them must have looked like an upside-down basket with two rows of spikes sticking up out of its back as it crawled upon the sand. Another was a swimming creature with five mushroom-shaped eyes and a single "arm" that was a long tube with a claw at the end. Still another seems so weird that it has been named *Hallucigenia*, meaning "imaginary dreamlike creature"! It had fourteen stiff spikelike legs, seven snakelike pincer-tipped tentacles on its back (each of which may have been a separate mouth!), and a lumpy ball at one end of its body and a curving tube at the other. Paleontologists don't know how this animal moved, how it ate, or which end of it was which!

The fossils of the Burgess Shale have been under study for more than eighty years, and paleontologists are still finding out new things from them. This certainly was one of the greatest discoveries in the history of paleontology.

Moving Continents, Shifting Seas

Look carefully on a map or globe at the east coast of South America and west coast of Africa, facing each other across the Atlantic Ocean, and you will see that they look very much as if they could fit together like pieces of a puzzle. In the early 1900s, a German astronomer and meteorologist named Alfred Wegener noticed this and began to ponder on it.

The plants and animals that live in South America are very different from those in Africa. But Wegener learned that in both countries a number of fossils of prehistoric plants and animals had been found that were identical to one another. These were creatures such as ferns and snails that could not easily have crossed the ocean in any way. Wegener came to the conclusion that when these creatures were alive, South America and Africa must have been joined together, and something had made them split apart.

This was a wild idea in the early 1900s. Geologists and other scientists regarded the surface of the earth as a single great shell of rock. It was believed that the continents, which are composed of fairly lightweight rock, were sunk deep into the much heavier rock forming the seabed, like icebergs floating in an ocean. Most geologists thought the continents moved up and

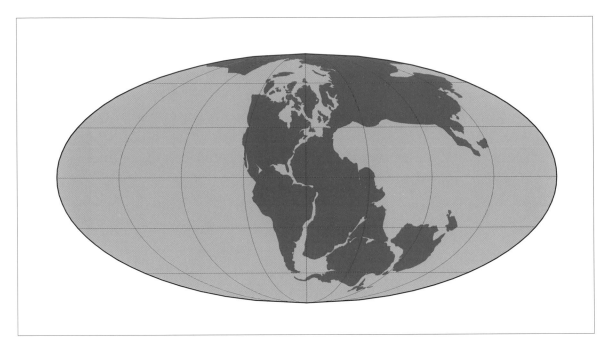

A computer-generated map of the world, 200 million years ago—just before the break up of Pangaea

down gradually, due to pressures from the hot molten rock far below, but no one even considered that they might move sideways, for that would have been impossible. As for why there were fossils of the same plants and animals on different continents, it was believed there had once been "bridges" of land between continents. Obviously, animals could have gone from one continent to another on these, and some of them might have had seeds of plants stuck to their fur or skin. The bridges no longer existed, it was explained, because they had eventually broken off and sunk down into the seabed.

Wegener did not agree with any of this. He had no doubt that the fossilized plants and animals had all lived on one piece of land, which had come apart after they had become fossils. In 1912, he presented this idea in two lectures to German scientific organizations. Most scientists felt that his ideas were ridiculous.

Wegener searched for evidence for his ideas, and in 1915 he published a book called *The Origin of Continents and Oceans*, which presented what he had found. He showed that if Africa and South America could be joined together at the edges of their continental shelves, where the land slopes down to the seabed, there are sections of very ancient rock at each edge that would fit together perfectly. He pointed out that there are mountain ranges and rock formations that would actually continue right from one continent to the other. He listed fossils of many identical animals and plants that are found on several widely separated continents, and explained why such creatures could not possibly have developed exactly the same, so far apart. Wegener insisted that there had once been a single gigantic supercontinent, which he called Pangaea (meaning "all the land"), and that this supercontinent had been split apart in some way.

But scientists pointed out a major problem with Wegener's idea. He could not explain why the supercontinent had come apart, could not suggest what kind of titanic force could have broken it into smaller pieces and then pushed the pieces away from one another. Largely because of this, most scientists continued to regard his idea as nothing but fantasy. Wegener died in 1930, during a scientific expedition to Greenland, still being scoffed at by scientists all over the world.

But today, we know that Alfred Wegener was mostly right. Even though most scientists of his time literally laughed at him, a few became interested in his ideas and began to consider them. More than thirty years after his death, Wegener's theory, which became known as continental drift, was proved right, and a whole new field of geology, known as plate tectonics, came into being. Wegener gave us a giant step forward in our understanding of the vast forces that are constantly reshaping the earth's surface.

6

AERONAUTICS-ASTRONAUTICS

For centuries, people dreamed of inventing a machine or device that would enable humans to fly. In 1783, such an invention finally appeared, when two Frenchmen, Jean François Pilâtre de Rozier and François d'Arlandes, made a flight over the city of Paris in a balloon filled with hot air. More than sixty years later in 1849, an Englishman named George Cayley built a winged craft out of cloth and wood that actually carried a small boy for a short distance through the air. This was the first "piloted" glider.

A balloon is called a lighter-than-air craft, because the substance that carries it into the sky—heated air or a gas such as hydrogen or helium—is actually lighter than air and will automatically rise upward. A glider, however, is what is called a heavier-than-air craft. It depends upon the wind to hold it up.

Neither a balloon nor a glider can be controlled very well. Both will go only wherever the wind blows them. So people became interested in finding some way of steering balloons and gliders, to make them flying devices that could be controlled. In 1852, a French inventor built a balloon shaped like a football and attached a platform with an engine and a propeller to it. This was the world's first airship—a lighter-than-air craft that could be steered. Many people thought this was the final answer to the age-old dream of being able to fly.

But there were a number of inventors who conceived of putting an engine on a man-carrying glider, to create a heavier-than-air "flying machine" that would be faster and easier to steer than a huge, clumsy airship. By the beginning of the twentieth century, a number of men had attempted to create a flying machine and had failed. Most people felt that such a thing was completely impossible. Nevertheless, a few dreamers continued to try.

The Beginning of the Airplane

It was a chilly December day in 1903. In the icy water of the Potomac River, not far from Washington, D.C., a houseboat lay at anchor. A device that resembled a winged dragonfly made of wood strips and cloth perched on a 70-foot (21-meter) railroad track built onto the houseboat's roof. A man sat in this machine, behind a purring gasoline engine and spinning propeller.

The man raised an arm and waved. Another man released a rope that held the machine in place. The winged machine sped smoothly down the track, reached the end of the houseboat, and shot out into the open air. Then it turned over and plunged straight down into the river. Another flying machine had failed.

Many such flying machines, as they were called, had been built during the last years of the nineteenth and the first few years of the twentieth centuries. None had worked, and most people did not believe there would ever be one that worked. A prominent scientist had written a magazine article explaining why it was actually impossible for a heavier-than-air craft to be able to fly. Once its forward speed slowed down, he pointed out, it would simply fall to the ground. There was nothing to make it stay in the air. However, on the very day in December when the flying machine from the houseboat fell into the Potomac River, two young men in North Carolina were putting the finishing touches on a heavier-than-air flying machine that they were absolutely sure would fly successfully. For years, Wilbur and Orville Wright had been studying and testing ways of getting a man-carrying, engine-powered glider to fly. They built models and tested them in a wind tunnel they invented. They built and flew gliders, constantly making improvements. One improvement allowed them to twist the glider's wings as it flew, so that it would stay on an even path. They also invented a device they called a horizontal rudder, which could make the glider climb and dive.

The Wright brothers had also studied the structures of many unsuccessful flying machines, and made an important discovery. All the propellers of the unsuccessful machines had been flat, like the blades of a windmill. Orville and Wilbur felt that a flying machine propeller should be like a pair of whirling wings, to pull the craft forward. They built their own propellers, putting a twist in them so they would pull at the air.

On December 14, they decided everything was ready. With the help of

Orville (left) and Wilbur (right) Wright, whose successful flights on December 17, 1903, marked the beginning of modern aviation

some men from nearby Kitty Hawk, North Carolina, they carried their craft from its storage shed to the hill from which they intended to take off. They had built a track 60 feet (18 meters) long down the side of the hill. The craft, named *Flyer*, was placed on a wheeled platform that would roll along the track.

The brothers flipped a coin to see who would make the flight. Wilbur won. He lay flat on his stomach on the lower wing, and started the engine. *Flyer* raced down the track, lifted off the wheeled platform, and rose some 15 feet (4.5 meters) into the air. It soared forward about 60 feet and sank to the ground, taking some slight damage.

The craft had flown, but 60 feet was not enough of a test. The brothers repaired the damage and were ready to try again on December 17. It was Orville's turn this time. He climbed onto *Flyer* and started it up. Wilbur ran alongside for a short distance, steadying the wing with one hand. Then *Flyer* lifted into the air and Orville saw the ground rushing past, 10 feet (3 meters) below him. The craft was definitely flying under its own power. It landed softly, about 120 feet (36 meters) from the end of the track.

This was the first true flight of a powered, piloted, heavier-than-air flying machine. The Wright brothers made three more flights that day, the longest one of 852 feet (259 meters). The importance of these flights was that *Flyer* had gotten into the air and stayed there under its own power, without the use of lighter-than-air gas, as an airship needed, or wind, as a glider required. This was the beginning of the kind of fast, efficient air flight that is now common—the beginning of a vastly changed world.

A Different Idea for Flight

In 1907, Paul Cornu, a French bicycle dealer, tested a heavier-than-air flying machine that he had designed and built. It was completely different from the Wright brothers' airplane. It had no wings, and it had two huge propellers that faced up toward the sky instead of facing forward. When Cornu sat down in the craft and turned on the engine, the propellers started to spin and the aircraft rose 1 foot (30 centimeters) straight up off the ground. It hovered at that height for twenty seconds, then dropped to the ground and broke apart.

Nevertheless, the flight had been a success. Cornu's machine was the world's first helicopter. He had shown that such a craft was possible, and in time it would become as common as the airplane.

THE "MOON MAN"

Robert Hutchings Goddard, an American from Massachusetts, began to think about spaceflight at the age of seventeen, four years before the Wright brothers even made their first successful airplane flight. At that time, of course, most people did not believe that airplane flight was possible, and as for spaceflight, people hardly thought about that at all. Most people, scientists included, did not even have any idea of how it might be done. The science fiction writer Jules Verne had written a book called *From the Earth to the Moon*, published in 1865, in which a spacecraft was shot to the moon out of an enormous cannon, and another writer, H. G. Wells, had conceived of a spacecraft made out of a metal that was not affected by gravity. Neither of these methods was possible, of course. But no one seemed to have any real understanding of how a spacecraft might actually be built and flown.

Goddard did, however. He understood that a spacecraft would have to operate on the same principle as a fireworks rocket. The blast of fire and hot gas that erupts from the back of a rocket actually pushes the rocket up into the air, and this is exactly how a spaceship must be launched. Also, once the craft is out in space, only a rocket blast could enable it to "fly" in a particular direction. No other kind of engine would work in space. Goddard understood this, and as a young college student he was experimenting with small rockets he built himself, testing to see how they might work in the airlessness of space.

By the time he had become a professor of physics at a small college, Goddard had determined that to have enough power to escape from earth's gravity and get into space, a rocket would have to use a high-energy fuel, such as liquid oxygen. He also worked out the idea of what would someday be known as a multiple-stage rocket—a number of extra fuel tanks would be attached to the craft, and could be fired one after another to provide the total amount of power needed. (In the late 1800s, a Russian schoolteacher named Konstantin Tsiolkovsky had first proposed such ideas, but no one had paid any attention to them, and Goddard had never heard of them.)

In 1919, Goddard wrote a report on everything he had worked out about

Robert Goddard, a pioneer in the study of rockets, contributed to the field until his death in 1945.

rockets over the years. He called it *A Method of Reaching Extreme Altitudes*. In it he suggested an experiment in which a small rocket could be sent to the moon and would explode a magnesium flare when it struck the moon's surface, producing a bright flash that could be seen from earth by telescope. This would show that the rocket had reached its goal. But in 1919, the idea of trying to send a rocket to the moon was ridiculous to most people. Most of the scientific and technical organizations that Goddard sent his report to paid no attention to it. However, some newspapers learned of it, and carried scornful stories jokingly referring to Goddard as the "moon man," and questioning his common sense.

However, Goddard's work helped to solve a lot of problems years later, when the United States began trying to build rocket engines for space vehicles. He is now honored as one of the pioneers of astronautics, the science of spaceflight.

Further Reading

Apfel, Necia. *It's All Relative.* New York: Lothrop, 1981.

Asimov, Isaac. *How Did We Find Out About Our Genes?* New York: Walker and Co., 1983.

Aylesworth, Thomas G. *Moving Continents: Our Changing Earth.* Hillside, N.J.: Enslow, 1990.

Byczynski, Lynn. *Genetics: Nature's Blueprints.* San Diego: Lucent Books, 1991.

Dunn, Andrew. *Marie Curie.* New York: Franklin Watts, 1991.

Goldenstern, Joyce. *Albert Einstein: Physicist and Genius.* Hillside, N.J.: Enslow, 1994.

Grady, Sean M. *Plate Tectonics: Earth's Shifting Crust.* San Diego: Lucent Books, 1991.

Jefferis, David. *Flight: Fliers and Flying Machines.* New York: Franklin Watts, 1994.

Lafferty, Peter. *Albert Einstein.* New York: Franklin Watts, 1992.

Lampton, Christopher. *Rocketry: From Goddard to Space Travel.* New York: Franklin Watts, 1988.

McGowen, Tom. *Radioactivity: From the Curies to the Atomic Age.* New York: Franklin Watts, 1986.

Milne, Lorus J., and Margery Milne. *Understanding Radioactivity.* New York: Macmillan, 1989.

Morgan, Nina. *Guglielmo Marconi.* New York: Franklin Watts, 1991.

Parker, Steve. *Marie Curie and Radium.* New York: HarperCollins, 1992.

Poynter, Margaret. *Marie Curie: Discoverer of Radium.* Hillside, N.J.: Enslow, 1994.

Reynolds, Quentin. *The Wright Brothers.* New York: Random House, 1981.

Streissguth, Tom. *Rocket Man: The Story of Robert Goddard.* Minneapolis: Carolrhoda, 1995.

Swisher, Clarice. *Albert Einstein.* San Diego: Lucent Books, 1994.

Tames, Richard. *The Wright Brothers.* New York: Franklin Watts, 1990.

Index

About the Author

Tom McGowen was born in Evanston, Illinois, reared in Chicago, and is a lifelong resident of the Chicago area. Married, he has four children and eleven grandchildren.

Mr. McGowen is the author of nearly fifty books for children and young adults, a body of work that includes both fiction (chiefly fantasy and science-fiction) and nonfiction. Two of his books have been named Outstanding Science Trade Books for Children; one has been selected as a Notable Children's Trade Book in the Field of Social Studies.

Mr. McGowen is a member of the Author's Guild, the Children's Reading Round Table, and the Society of Midland Authors.